⊞ ... IT IS QUITE IMPOSSIBLE
TO CONSIDER THE BUILDING AS
ONE THING AND ITS FURNISHINGS
ANOTHER, ITS SETTING AND
ENVIRONMENT STILL ANOTHER.
IN THE SPIRIT IN WHICH THESE
BUILDINGS ARE CONCEIVED,
THESE ARE ALL ONE THING,
TO BE FORESEEN AND PROVIDED
FOR IN THE NATURE OF THE
STRUCTURE. ⊞

— FRANK LLOYD WRIGHT

AUSGEFÜHRTE BAUTEN UND
ENTWÜRFE VON
FRANK LLOYD WRIGHT, 1910

# FRANK LLOYD WRIGHT'S
# FURNISHINGS

⁜ CARLA LIND ⁜

AN ARCHETYPE PRESS BOOK
POMEGRANATE ARTBOOKS, SAN FRANCISCO

Library of Congress Cataloging-in-Publication Data

Lind, Carla.

Frank Lloyd Wright's furnishings / Carla Lind.

    p.    cm.    — (Wright at a glance)

"An Archetype Press book."

Includes bibliographical references.

ISBN 0-87654-471-5

1. Wright, Frank Lloyd, 1867–1959 — Criticism and interpretation. 2. Architect-designed furniture — United States. I. Title. II. Series: Lind, Carla. Wright at a glance.

NA2439.W75L56 1995                                     95-420

749.213—dc20                                             CIP

Published by

Pomegranate

Box 808022

Petaluma, California

94975-8022

Catalogue no. A799

Produced by Archetype Press, Inc.

Project Director: Diane Maddex

Editorial Assistants:

Gretchen Smith Mui, Kristi Flis,

and Christina Hamme

Designer: Robert L. Wiser

10  9  8  7  6  5  4  3

Printed in Singapore

Opening photographs: Page 1: Frank Lloyd Wright at Taliesin, 1924. Page 2: A tall-back chair at the Hollyhock house (1917) in Hollywood. Pages 6–7: "Blue loggia" at Taliesin, with barrel chairs and other Wright furniture.

# CONTENTS

FRANK LLOYD WRIGHT (1867-1959) was a product of his time. Had he been born in another era, his architecture undoubtedly would have been different. His proclaimed beliefs in simplicity, nature, unity, and the arts in the service of architecture were all based on common ideas of the mid-nineteenth and early twentieth centuries. Ralph Waldo Emerson, Viollet-le-Duc, Owen Jones, John Ruskin, William Morris, and Walt Whitman were among the most well known purveyors of these messages. Leaders of the Arts and Crafts movement published their own magazines as early as 1893, promoting their theories, their designs, and their products.

For Wright, this profusion of ideas reinforced the teachings of his mother. They gave deeper meaning to the Froebel kindergarten training of his childhood, which had taught him to distill nature—to find its geometric essence. Wright's personal formulation of what he called organic architecture was a hybrid of these influences, enriched by a fascination with Japanese simplicity and modularity. Wright's style was given final form during his apprenticeship with Louis Sullivan from 1888 to 1892.

The shapes and colors of the furnishings and art glass in the living room of the Robie house (1906), Chicago, repeat its architectural forms. The sofa's shape, for example, echoes the ceiling above. The furniture trim matches the moldings on the surrounding walls.

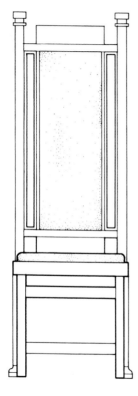

A Robie house chair (left) is one of Wright's classic Prairie Style forms. At Taliesin (1911–59), his own home in Wisconsin, Wright integrated his art collection into the living room design (opposite).

How he applied these concepts, transforming them from words into substance, was his genius. Nowhere are his artistry and his understanding of the principles inherent in nature revealed more than in the decorative arts designed during his seventy-year career. Childhood lessons with the Froebel blocks taught him about abstraction, the relationship of parts to the whole, and the discipline of working on a grid. This gave him the methodology he needed to create the many interrelated elements of each commission. Just as his father composed music, Wright sat with his T-square and triangle and composed buildings — first the major movements, then the minor ones, each building on the other, all flowing from a common source.

To Wright, organic architecture meant that a building grew from within: from the nature of the site, the nature of the materials, and the nature of the clients' needs. A pivotal component of his design philosophy was the inclusion of decorative elements, fixed and free-standing, as parts of the architectural whole. His buildings were not neutral shells but multidimensional, intricate

compositions for living, working, and worshiping. Nature remained his greatest source of inspiration. Wright's decorative designs grew from a building's nature just as leaves and blossoms grow from a tree.

A motif for an object would often evolve from the drawings for its building, repeating or expanding on a pattern or detail. Unity prevailed throughout—from wall elevation to art glass window, from floor plan to carpet, from wood banding to table leg.

The number of pieces he designed for clients varied. In some early commissions, there were only a few built-in cabinets or a table, in addition to art glass and other integral ornament. But gradually Wright persuaded a greater number of clients to grant him more control. If allowed, he would design all the cabinets and upholstered furniture, attached and freestanding lighting, fireplace hardware, table linens, and carpets. To complete his composition, he was even known to design clothing for the woman of the house. His objective was simplicity, unity, and harmony. From this would come repose, which Wright saw as a necessary component of a good home.

⠿ Frustrated by the lifeless architecture and decorative products derived from historic forms and produced by machine, nineteenth century design theorists undertook a search for a style more characteristic of the age of science and knowledge. The detailed study of natural phenomena and organic forms became a nineteenth century preoccupation. ⠿

David A. Hanks
*The Decorative Designs of Frank Lloyd Wright,* 1979

Isabel Martin's dress, believed to be Wright's design, was seen as part of the composition of her Prairie Style home (1904) in Buffalo, New York.

WRIGHT WAS NOT ONLY THE COMPOSER
of symphony-like buildings; he was the orchestra conductor as well. Because a single commission called for dozens of individual designs, it was impossible for one person to do it all. He thus depended on other designers in his studio and a few trusted artists and outside contractors to carry out his plans. From his early years in Oak Park, Illinois, and later at the Taliesin Fellowship, he surrounded himself with devoted followers he trained to become "the fingers on his hand."

    Wright's involvement in details was significant, but it varied from commission to commission. During the busiest Prairie Style years (1904–9), he depended on a talented designer, George Niedecken, to implement some of his most celebrated interiors. Niedecken began with renderings and murals for Wright clients and eventually participated in twelve Wright commissions including the Dana-Thomas, Coonley, Robie, May, Bogk, and Allen houses. Following Wright's lead, like selected other associates, he could share design responsibilities, be an intermediary with clients, do working drawings, contract for the manufacture of items, and oversee installation.

From dining chairs to print tables, rectilinear furnishings defined different activities at the Dana-Thomas house (1902) in Springfield, Illinois.

**Simplicity**

Pure, honest presentation of forms and materials

**Integral ornament**

Decorative features that are not applied but derive from a building's structure and materials

**Parts of the whole**

Components that have individual beauty and fine proportion when viewed alone but become more important as parts of the whole

**Coordinated furniture**

Built-in features such as window seats and sideboards to conserve space. Freestanding pieces that relate and often have multiple uses

**Nature motifs**

Stylized natural forms drawn from plants and flowers—more conventional early, more abstract later on

**Basic geometric shapes**

Two and three dimensions used to devise patterns and forms

**Shared grammar**

Repetition of a theme throughout a building to create unity

**Sturdy construction**

Solid, well-built furniture, frequently of oak in the early years

**Fine craftsmanship**

Association with fine artisans. Artistry in crafting individual decorative elements

**Natural materials**

Shaping and finishing selected to reveal the inherent nature of the materials

**Natural colors**

Warm natural colors like those of a sunny autumn day in the Midwest—golds, browns, rusty oranges, and yellow-greens. Cherokee red and metallic gold used as accents

**Innovative lighting**

Concealed fixtures in light decks, geometric lamps, art glass panels

**Multiple arts**

Sculpture, painting, and metalwork chosen to enhance the architecture

**Human scale**

Pieces sized to a particular space, whether large or small, and related to human proportions

Top: Integrated art and furnishings at Taliesin West and a Richard Bock sculpture at the Dana-Thomas house. Bottom: Modular Usonian furniture and an oak Prairie Style screen.

# BUILT-IN FURNITURE

UNITY AND EFFICIENCY

▓ Arrangements for the infor-
mality of sitting comfortably,
singly or in groups, where it is
desirable or natural to sit, and
still to belong in disarray to the
scheme as a whole—that is a
matter difficult to accomplish. ▓
Frank Lloyd Wright
Kahn Lectures, 1930

For his Oak Park home,
Wright designed built-in
seating beneath the living
room bay window and in the
fireplace inglenook. The
original dining area had a
polygonal cabinet that
echoed the bays nearby.

WRIGHT'S FIRST FURNITURE DESIGNS
were for built-in cabinets and seating. Throughout his career he favored this technique for integrating furniture
with the architecture. It was efficient, orderly, and eco-
nomical as well as stylistically unifying.

Some of the earliest examples can be found in his
own Oak Park home (1889), which Wright used as a lab-
oratory for his experiments in comfortable living. Repeating the grammar of the house, they were constructed
of the same materials—their continuity adding spacious-
ness to the small rooms in ways that freestanding pieces
could not have achieved. Sideboards of the period such as
at the McArthur (1892) and Heller (1896) houses in
Chicago had delicate art glass doors.

Wright's mature Usonian houses continued the
tradition with built-in seats beneath windows and bookshelves—offering seating like an extended arm. Even his
later residences such as the Brown house (1949), Kala-
mazoo, Michigan, had built-in cabinets, bookshelves, and
long seating areas (page 16). The harmony of these spaces
would have been disturbed with store-bought furniture.

❖ The details of the house are as much in their place and as consistent in themselves and in relation to each other, as the whole house is to the surroundings. ❖

Robert C. Spencer, Jr.
"The Work of
Frank Lloyd Wright,"
*Architectural Review,* 1900

Simple upholstery fabrics on the built-in furniture at Fallingwater (1935), Mill Run, Pennsylvania, provide a background for specialty textiles, including pillows, throws, and carpets—as well as a foil for nature's own patterns.

# FREE STANDING FURNITURE

## PARTS OF THE BUILDING ITSELF

▦ I tried to make my clients see that furniture and furnishings . . . should be seen as minor parts of the building itself, even if detached or kept aside to be used on occasion. ▦
Frank Lloyd Wright
Kahn Lectures, 1930

George Niedecken's designs for the Irving house (1909), Decatur, Illinois, included a combined oak table and couch. The house, completed in 1913 by Marion Mahony and Hermann von Holst, was the last Wright designed before he left his practice for Europe.

A NATURAL EVOLUTION OF HIS belief in unified compositions for living were Wright's designs for individual pieces. It pained him to see clients move their old furniture into his new houses.

Beginning with dining rooms, Wright offered his own compatible elements. Dining chairs, in response to the rectangular geometry of his Prairie Style houses, were tall, straight, and strong. Other designers of the time—C.F.A. Voysey, M. H Baillie Scott, and Charles Rennie Mackintosh—were also creating interiors that drew on simplicity and nature. All simultaneously developed their versions of tall-back chairs. Wright's tables were sturdy, straightforward, and simple, repeating the detail of a room's oak moldings. The Dana-Thomas house (1902) included nearly a hundred furniture designs, while others received only a library table or dining room furniture.

The cabinetmakers responsible for the fine craftsmanship in the Prairie years, such as John Ayers, Harris Mill, Matthews Brothers, and F. H. Bresler, were frequently replaced later on by clients or carpenters who built Wright's simple Usonian furniture on the site.

The barrel chair design seen at Taliesin (right) was also used at Wingspread (1937), Racine, Wisconsin.

Usually modular so that it could be grouped in different combinations, the plywood construction of Wright's Usonian furniture was an extension of the walls around it. Pieces often conformed to the specific geometric module used for a building's design— square, rectangular, triangular, or hexagonal. Clockwise from the left are chairs created for Taliesin West, the Sondern and Trier Usonian houses, and the Price Tower, a hexagonal aluminum design.

# BEDROOM FURNITURE

TWO DECADES AFTER DESIGNING his first bedroom furniture, for his own house in Oak Park, Wright produced a master bedroom (1908) for the haberdasher Meyer May in Grand Rapids, Michigan. It was fitted with twin oak beds, a dresser, and a costumer for laying out clothes. At a time when most clothes were stored folded, Wright specially outfitted built-in closets with innovative pull-out hanger rods. The adjoining morning room was equipped with a dressing table, a lounge chair, and a large dresser—all designed as modules of this totally unified, state-of-the-art suite.

At Fallingwater (1935), Mill Run, Pennsylvania, beds seem to grow from the stone walls, and desks and shelves are cantilevered like the balconies over the waterfall. Furniture edges repeat the curve of the concrete parapets beyond. Bedrooms in the Usonian houses that followed were usually tiny. Their beds were based on each house's module, so some had to be custom made. The triangular module of the Palmer house (1950), Ann Arbor, Michigan, dictated parallelogram-shaped beds. Cabinets and desks were usually built in to further conserve space.

Fitting neatly into the geometry of the room, standard rectangular forms at his Oak Park home (1889–1909) suited Wright's vocabulary of the time. Integrating the arts, he also had stencils and murals by Orlando Giannini applied to the walls. Built-in cabinets and closets between rooms saved space and provided a sound buffer.

▓ Sleeping rooms should be as pleasant as the living rooms and should be so arranged that the second floor is a natural development of the first. ▓

Frank Lloyd Wright
"The Architect and the Machine," 1894

Meyer May's Wright-designed bedroom was fitted out with custom beds, dressers, and chairs, as well as a costumer, matching bed linens, and even a one-of-a-kind, rectilinear gas log for the fireplace.

⠿ Why should your second floor be less carefully planned than [the] first floor! Are you to pay more respect to the neighbors than to yourself, then perhaps your underclothing is shabby when your hat and coat are fine. ⠿

Frank Lloyd Wright
"The Architect and the Machine," 1894

# SPECIALTY PIECES

## CUSTOM-DESIGNED TREASURES

A special desk was designed for Queene Ferry Coonley's house (1907), Riverside, Illinois. Built-in light fixtures unified normally separate functions, a feat that Wright achieved with attached light standards on some of his dining room tables.

THE MORE FREEDOM THE CLIENT gave Wright, the more he moved beyond the basics, venturing into unusual pieces. Believing a house to be a machine for living, his designs responded to the specific use that a piece was meant to serve. The print table that Wright designed in 1902 for Susan Lawrence Dana (page 15) and the Littles of Peoria, Illinois, was hinged so that it could be used in various forms and folded away when not needed. Because it was perfectly suited for displaying Japanese prints, Wright—an avid collector—had one made for his own home as well.

Lucille and Isadore Zimmerman, like Wright, loved music and often held recitals in the garden room of their Manchester, New Hampshire, house (1950). While visiting Taliesin, they saw a quartet stand and asked Wright to design one for them as well. Its geometry and materials suit the space while serving a useful purpose. Wright's office also provided designs for at least two piano cases, one for the Frickes (1901) in Oak Park and one for the Ambergs (1909) in Grand Rapids, Michigan. The latter was probably designed by Marion Mahony or George Niedecken after Wright had departed for Europe.

· · · · · · · · · · · · · · · · · · · · · · · · · · · · · · · 31

# COMMERCIAL DESIGNS

## FURNISHINGS FOR WORK

THREE OF WRIGHT'S MOST INNOVATIVE commissions were for office buildings. His response to each was thoroughly original and involved extensive custom designs for furnishings. Metal desks and cabinets for the revolutionary Larkin Building (1903, demolished), Buffalo, New York, were specially designed. Paper handling in this mail-order company made efficiency a priority. Some desk chairs were hinged, without legs, to ease the nightly cleaning. Others were on a pedestal with rollers and an adjustable back. Made by Van Dorn Iron Works, all were designed using the building's rectilinear grammar.

Steelcase manufactured Wright's designs for the Johnson Wax buildings (1936–44), Racine, Wisconsin. The exposure to Wright's philosophy was inspirational to the company, causing executives to think more about color in office furniture as well as more creative designs.

Furniture for the Price Tower (1952), Bartlesville, Oklahoma, used a triangle. From the building's parallelogram module grew hexagonal chairs (page 25) and custom-shaped desks. The colorful furnishings are integral to the wide-angled spaces they populate.

⊞ Wright wanted the furniture to reflect the columns' treatment of the cantilevers, round surfaces and light base supports. Desks of the 1930's had large bases to protect the floor but Wright wanted desk legs to narrow at the base. ⊞

Jonathan Lipman
*Frank Lloyd Wright and the Johnson Wax Buildings*, 1986

The streamlined forms of the red desks at the Johnson Wax Building, some with built-in filing systems, repeated the architectural lines. The three-legged tubular chairs proved hazardous and have been replaced with a four-legged version.

## LAMPS AND LANTERNS

### DESIGNS FOR THE ELECTRIC AGE

▓ No glaring fixtures there, but light, incorporated in the wall, which sifts from behind its surface opening appropriately in tremulous pattern, as sunlight sifts through leaves in the trees. ▓

Frank Lloyd Wright
"Architect, Architecture, and the Client," 1896

An early version of this square table lamp, with a shade hanging from a cantilevered arm, was first seen at Midway Gardens in 1914. Its shade was sometimes fitted with rice paper, like this one at Taliesin West (1937–59), Scottsdale, Arizona. Others had Japanese patterned paper shades.

WRIGHT LOVED TO PLAY WITH LIGHT, both natural and artificial, and preferred broken light from above. The introduction of electricity just as he was beginning his practice brought new opportunities for distributing light around a building. Safer than gas, electric light could be concealed or brought closer to where it was needed.

Wright designed numerous art glass light fixtures for walls, ceilings, and table tops, usually several styles for a given building. All were geometric, often in a shape different from the predominant one. He placed light overhead behind art glass panels in many of his Prairie Style houses, often in entry halls but in living and dining room ceilings as well. The filtered light passing through the golds and greens of the translucent panels dissolved the solidity of the ceiling—creating a mystery about the source of the light. Was it daylight or artificial light?

The three-dimensional patterns of his California textile-block houses from the 1920s were sometimes pierced, so that glass or light bulbs could be inserted to create subtle, broken-light patterns. Like the lighting for his Usonian houses, it was integral to each building's design.

Lamps came with double pedestals (at the second Little house of 1912 in Minnesota, above) and single pedestals (at the Dana-Thomas house, left). Fixtures on cabinets and decks helped make Wright's houses glow with indirect light.

# CARPETS AND FABRICS

## NATURAL WEAVES, NATURAL COLORS

FOR SOME CONSENTING CLIENTS, custom carpets continued the prevailing unity of their Wright-designed environments. Multiple rugs were woven for several of the Prairie Style and transitional houses, including the Dana-Thomas, Robie, May, Coonley, Heurtley, Bogk, and Hollyhock residences. Special sizes were woven for each space. Most had an earthy solid ground and small amounts of geometric pattern, a linear border, or medallions. Designs related to other motifs in the building and resembled an elongated shadow or a reflection from a nearby art glass window—jewels of light that had landed on the floor. Similar to Wright's glass designs, the carpets introduced an accent color—a touch of red, blue, mauve, or green—to set off the soft, warm color schemes.

Twelve hundred carpets and various patterned textiles were reportedly woven in China for the Imperial Hotel (1915, demolished) in Tokyo. The magnificent design for the banquet hall was an abstraction of a giant peacock. Later carpets, such as those for his son David Wright's circular house (1950) in Phoenix, were bolder abstractions, brighter in color.

Chevron shapes and abstracted plant forms were combined with linear elements to create sixteen carpet patterns for the May house (1908). Sixty-seven drawings of various furnishings were found in the designer George Niedecken's files for the house.

Until 1955, when Wright introduced a line of fabrics for Schumacher (Design 104 is shown on pages 40–41), he had created few patterned textiles. He preferred solid, simple weaves. In the early years he often specified velvets or mohair satin in soft earthen colors. Later on he used handwoven fabrics.

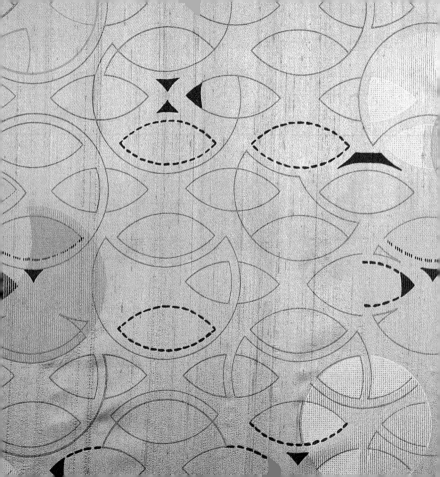

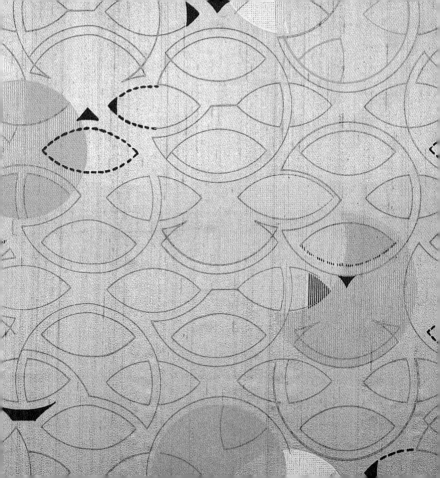

## W O O D E N  P A N E L S

### S C R E E N S  O F  L I G H T  A N D  S H A D E

Wright designed fret-sawn panels for his Oak Park home (above) and the Roberts house fireplace (opposite).

BEGINNING EARLY IN HIS CAREER, in his Oak Park home, Wright devised fret-sawn wooden panels as a way to break areas of light in a natural way. Stylized leafy patterns over translucent rice paper—reminiscent of Louis Sullivan but simpler, more geometric, and less floral—covered recessed lighting in the ceilings of both his dining room and children's playroom (1895). In other early commissions in the Chicago area, such as the Harlan (1892, demolished), Winslow (1894), and remodeled Charles Roberts (1896) residences, Wright used cut wooden panels as integral ornament inside and outside.

Abandoning the technique for many years, Wright returned to it in the 1930s in his Usonian houses. The patterns became even simpler—purely geometric but playful angular cutouts in plywood panels that commonly covered clerestory windows. They were an inexpensive way to create ornament and break light entering a space. Like art glass windows in the Prairie Style houses, cutout panels provided a frame for the natural views outside. Interesting shadows on the walls and floors repeated the rhythm of a house, contributing to the harmonious feeling.

❖ How lovely this wood to the touch, grateful to the eye, in reality the beauty of the wood, silken and soft it is with the sheen of a flower petal. ❖
Frank Lloyd Wright
"Architect, Architecture, and the Client," 1896

Layers of perforated, geometric clerestory panels were placed above built-in seating in the Gordon house (1956–64), Wilsonville, Oregon. They contribute a lacy lightness to the concrete block house.

# RELIEF PANELS

## FRIEZES AND TEXTILE BLOCKS

LOUIS SULLIVAN EDUCATED WRIGHT in the use of integral ornament, drawn from a building's materials and using its inherent properties. He objected to ornament that was applied to a building and not organic in origin. Sullivan was particularly adept at creating rich surfaces of terra cotta and plaster. Wright followed his lead in ornamental friezes for the exteriors of the Winslow (1894), Heller (1896), and Dana-Thomas (1902) houses and the Francisco Terrace (1895) and Francis (1895) apartment buildings, all in Illinois. More restrained than his *lieber Miester's* fluid designs, the patterns drew on botanical sources but were stylized and ordered.

As his designs became more abstract, Wright began using cut stone, a tighter material with sharper edges. The richly ornamented Imperial Hotel (1915) in Tokyo had several fireplace surrounds of relief panels of cut Oya stone combined with colorful murals. During the same period, Wright designed a cut-stone overmantel for the living room fireplace at the Hollyhock house (1917) in Hollywood. It incorporated the stylized flower ornament used elsewhere within the abstract composition.

**In a structure conceived in the organic sense, the ornamentation is conceived in the very ground plan, and is of the very constitution of the structure.**
Frank Lloyd Wright
*Ausgeführte Bauten und Entwürfe von Frank Lloyd Wright,* 1910

Wright's California textile-block designs, like those in the Ennis house (1923), Los Angeles, were made of cast, not cut, concrete and added a unique texture to the houses.

The intricate rectilinear designs related to the module, or grid, of each house.

## FENCES AND OBJETS D'ART

As he experimented with copper, Wright developed two of his finest handmade objects. One was a tall, narrow weed holder (right), the other a large round urn (opposite). Both featured simple geometric shapes in an embossed relief pattern made by James Miller. First seen before 1900, they appear in early photographs taken in his own studio.

WRIGHT WAS NOT SIMPLY AN ARCHITECT. He was also a designer. No utilitarian item was beyond his interest. A charter member of the Chicago Society of Arts and Crafts, Wright differed from other Arts and Crafts proponents in believing that the machine was a perfect partner for the simple geometric forms they all preferred.

Sheet metal, especially copper, was particularly suited to machine forming, and Wright used it for items such as vases. The earliest Wright-designed cast-iron fireplace andirons were for the Bradley (1900) and Davenport (1901) houses in Illinois, but others like those for the Lake Geneva Hotel (1911, demolished) followed.

Wright designed metal gates to define the beginning of a building—introducing a built object as a foil to the natural setting. Wrought-iron entrance gates for the Francis apartments (1895) and the Robie house (1906) in Chicago were early examples. Taliesin (1911–59) and Taliesin West (1937–59) have had several gates, as do a few of his later houses. Restrained, modular, and geometric, they express the prevailing design motifs of the buildings in yet another material and manner.

## CHINA, GLASS, AND SILVER

### DESIGNING FOR DINING

THE ENTIRE EXPERIENCE OF DINING, short of the food itself, was a concern of Wright's. During his career he designed intimate and public dining rooms, dining furniture, murals and lighting for dining areas, table linens, china, and silver service. Each element represented an opportunity for unifying and celebrating the ritual, for creating complete harmony.

The two greatest opportunities for a total dining environment have both been demolished. Because of financial difficulties, many of the decorative elements Wright designed for Midway Gardens (1913), an entertainment complex in Chicago, were not produced. But the china was, its heavy white forms encircled with a linked row of red squares—like frozen notes in a musical score.

The Imperial Hotel (1915) in Tokyo had two Wright-designed china patterns and a custom silver service. The gold-rimmed formal dinnerware used elements of the clustered square designs seen in the hotel's stonework, while overlapping circles played on the informal pattern. The seven-piece silver service called on the hexagonal shapes used in the Imperial furniture.

⊞ Decoration is intended to make Use more charming and Comfort more appropriate or a privilege has been abused. ⊞
Frank Lloyd Wright
*An Autobiography,* 1932

The table at the Lovness studio (1955), Stillwater, Minnesota, is set with china designed for the Imperial Hotel. Closely related to other Wright graphic designs of the period, it recalls murals at Midway Gardens, the Coonley Playhouse windows (1912) in Riverside, Illinois, and *Liberty* magazine covers (1927), all of which used overlapping circular forms in clear colors.

# SCULPTURE

## ART IN THE SERVICE OF ARCHITECTURE

▓ Nothing could go on unless
Wright had a finger in the pie. ▓
Richard W. Bock
*Memoirs of an American Artist
Sculptor, 1989*

Wright used sculpture inside
and out. Among other works,
Richard Bock helped create
the stork panels located at
the entrance to Wright's Oak
Park studio (opposite) and
the *Flower in a Crannied Wall*
statue (page 16) for the Dana-
Thomas house (1902); he
also collaborated with Marion
Mahony on the "moon-
children" fountain there.

IN THE SPIRIT OF THE TIME, WRIGHT
was an advocate for using the arts to serve architecture.
Throughout his career, he called on talented artists to enhance his buildings. The executed works seem to be the sole
design of neither Wright nor the artist but the result of a
tight collaboration between sympathetic, creative minds.

Before affiliating with contemporary artists, Wright
used casts of classical sculpture in his home. Nike, the
winged goddess, graced many of his early photographs,
and a Hellenistic frieze surrounds his entry hall. The two
crouched figures that flank his studio entrance (1898)
were executed by his friend and frequent collaborator
Richard Bock, with whom he worked for twenty years.
After moving to Buffalo, Bock did the monumental stone
carvings for the Larkin Building (1903) and two statues
for the Darwin Martin garden (1904).

Working with Alfonso Ianelli, a young Italian artist,
Wright modeled numerous clay forms cast in concrete for
Midway Gardens. Together they created the well-known
sprite figures. Said Bock: "It was an artist's gigantic dream,
fresh, vital, forceful and full of imagery."

# MURALS AND MOSAICS

WRIGHT FIRST COLLABORATED WITH Orlando Giannini in his Oak Park home, employing the artist to paint murals of Indians on both ends of his bedroom (page 26) and the *Genii and the Fisherman* over the playroom fireplace. His art glass work with Wright included fireplace mosaics for the Husser (1899), Darwin Martin (1904), and Ennis (1923) houses. It is believed that another versatile artist, Blanche Ostertag, designed at least two of these using iridescent glass tiles to create an airy wisteria design in gold, white, green, and pink.

George Niedecken assisted Wright with many of the Prairie Style interiors. Beginning with the mural of sumac, asters, and goldenrod for the Dana-Thomas house dining room (1902), he completed known murals for the Coonley, May, Amberg, and Irving residences.

Eugene Masselink, Wright's secretary for many years, was also an accomplished artist who designed abstract murals, screens, and door panels for many of Wright's 1950s commissions. Colorful triangular forms enlivened works at the Price Tower (1952) in Oklahoma and houses for the Price family and others.

▓ "Architect", "painter", "sculptor", "poet", "homemaker" working together in full accord to swell the modern harmony. ▓
Frank Lloyd Wright
"Architect, Architecture, and the Client," 1896

George Neidecken's hollyhock mural separates the hall and dining room of the May house (1908) in Grand Rapids, distilling the golds and greens of the house's palette. The extent of Wright's concern for the totality of a building design seemed to show no bounds.

• • • • • • • • • • • • • • • • • • • • • • • •

Brooks, H. Allen. *The Prairie School.* Toronto: University of Toronto Press, 1972.

Dunham, Judith. *Details of Frank Lloyd Wright.* San Francisco: Chronicle Books, 1994.

Hanks, David A. *The Decorative Designs of Frank Lloyd Wright.* New York: Dutton, 1979.

———. *Frank Lloyd Wright: Preserving an Architectural Heritage.* New York: Dutton, 1989.

Kaplan, Wendy. *The Art That Is Life: The Arts and Crafts Movement in America, 1875–1920.* Museum of Fine Arts. Boston: New York Graphic Society, 1987.

Lind, Carla. *The Wright Style.* New York: Simon and Schuster, 1992.

Manson, Grant Carpenter. *Frank Lloyd Wright to 1910: The First Golden Age.* New York: Van Nostrand Reinhold, 1958.

Pfeiffer, Bruce Brooks, ed. *Frank Lloyd Wright Monographs.* 12 vols. Tokyo: ADA Edita, 1987–88.

Robertson, Cheryl. *The Domestic Scene (1897–1927): George M. Niedecken, Interior Architect.* Milwaukee: Milwaukee Art Museum, 1981.

The author wishes to thank Penny Fowler, Frank Lloyd Wright Foundation; Meg Klinkow, Frank Lloyd Wright Home and Studio Foundation Research Center; Terry Marvel, Milwaukee Art Museum Prairie Archives; Steelcase Inc.; and the generous owners of the buildings included here. Special appreciation is due Mary and Lars Lofgren for assistance with new photography.

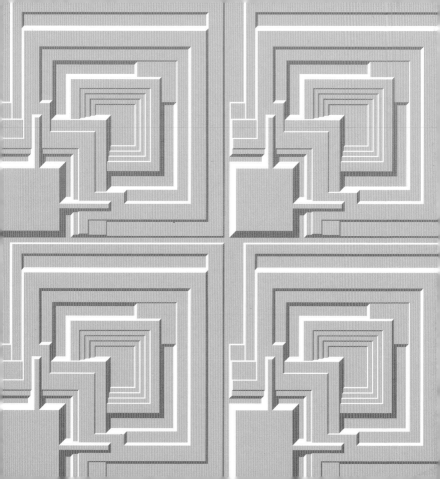